Young Writers

2004 POETRY COMP

ONCE A RHYME

IMAGINATION FOR
A NEW GENERATION

Somerset

Edited by Steve Twelvetree

 Young**Writers**

First published in Great Britain in 2005 by:
Young Writers
Remus House
Coltsfoot Drive
Peterborough
PE2 9JX
Telephone: 01733 890066
Website: www.youngwriters.co.uk

SB ISBN 1 84460 707 0

Foreword

Young Writers was established in 1991 and has been passionately devoted to the promotion of reading and writing in children and young adults ever since. The quest continues today. Young Writers remains as committed to engendering the fostering of burgeoning poetic and literary talent as ever.

This year's Young Writers competition has proven as vibrant and dynamic as ever and we are delighted to present a showcase of the best poetry from across the UK. Each poem has been carefully selected from a wealth of *Once Upon A Rhyme* entries before ultimately being published in this, our twelfth primary school poetry series.

Once again, we have been supremely impressed by the overall high quality of the entries we have received. The imagination, energy and creativity which has gone into each young writer's entry made choosing the best poems a challenging and often difficult but ultimately hugely rewarding task - the general high standard of the work submitted amply vindicating this opportunity to bring their poetry to a larger appreciative audience.

We sincerely hope you are pleased with our final selection and that you will enjoy *Once Upon A Rhyme Somerset* for many years to come.

Contents

Shannon Toop (10)   39
Lucy O'Shea (10)   40
Nicholas Batts (10)   41
Ricky Dean (10)   42
Luke Baker (10)   43
Hannah Daniel (9)   44
Chloe Oaten (9)   45
Matthew O'Shea (9)   46
Jessica Scott (9)   47

Charlton Mackrell CE Primary School
Laura Sandford (9)   48
Marcus Pile (9)   49
Oliver Alexander (9)   50
Yasmin India Wolfe (8)   51
Tristan Goldsmid (9)   52
Charlotte-Clare Wisniewski (8)   53
Charlotte Jane Male (9)   54
Sophie Baker (10)   55
Abigail Jane Smart (9)   56
Alice Achard (10)   57
Sean Webster (9)   58
Samantha Lucy chucher (10)   59
Nathan Harris (9)   60
Catherine May Baynes (9)   61
Mitchel William Newbury (10)   62
Michael James Male (11)   63
Jonathan Girt (9)   64
Kirsti Rendall (8)   65
Lee Parsons (10)   66
Josh Rydon (9)   67

Chilthorne Domer Church School
Katy Aldridge (9)   68
Cassandra Broadbent (10)   69
Jessica Baker (9)   70
Timothy Batstone (9)   71
Elise Burt (9)   72
Jasmine Burton (10)   73
Jessica Bushell (10)   74
Jemma Callow (9)   75

Ryan Coombes (10)	76
Jade Frost (10)	77
Chloe Giles (9)	78
Georgia Green (9)	79
Aaron Baker (10)	80
Jordon Higgins (9)	81
Rebecca Pearce (9) & Taela Horrigan (10)	82
Megan Johnson (9)	83
Adam Webber (9)	84
Jack Sharp (10)	85
Liam Parsons (10)	86
Lloyd Kannair & Leon Mahoney (10)	87
Natasha Jones (10)	88
Megan Knight (10)	89
Jessica Ogden (10)	90
Amy Wroot (10)	91
Tia Shrimpton (9)	92

Curry Mallet CE Primary School

Hannah Derrick (8)	93
Alex Manu (10)	94
Sam Murray (10)	95
Zoë Sanders (8)	96
Brandon Payn (8)	97
Ella Sanders (11)	98
Larissa Charlesworth (10)	99
Maisy Bond (9)	100
Molly Welch (10)	101
Michael Albrow (9)	102
Esme Hebditch (9)	103
Harriet Roberts (9)	104
Oliver Lucas (9)	105
Jenna Sparks (9)	106
Harry Dibble (9)	107
Sophia Eminson (9)	108
Kya Robson (9)	109
Ebony Cossey (9)	110
David Troutt (9)	111
Dominic Slade (9)	112

Kingsbury Episcopi Primary School

Daisy Baggs (10)	113
Josh Smith (10)	114
Grace Green (10)	115
Brad Cole (10)	116
Daniel Brain (11)	117
Jacob Ralph (9)	118
Tom Moore (10)	119
Callum Corbett (10)	120
Ieshia Rashbrook (9)	121
Alice Miller (9)	122
Honor Elliott (10)	123
Briannie Faull (10)	124
Chris Glyde (10)	125
Charlotte Gilliam (10)	126
Sam Reed (9)	127
Laurel Dyer (9)	128
William Stainer (9)	129
Kyle Butler (10)	130
Hannah Stuckey (10)	131
Jordan Cave (9)	132

Lancaster House School

Steven Wride (10)	133
Charlotte Perry (10)	134
Cara Williams (9)	135
Sam James (10)	136
Zoë Rose Howell (11)	137
Sophie Mussett (9)	138
Ben Emsley-Frake (10)	139

Monteclefe CE (VA) Junior School

Charlotte White (10)	140
Alexander Mitchell (11)	141
Philippa Cattle (10)	142
Matthew Haines (10)	143
Ashley Lazenbury (10)	144
Kyran Robinson (9)	145
Ashley Francis (10)	146
John Gay (10)	147

Rosie Billenness (10)	148
Vicky Foyne (11)	149
Samuel Stevens (10)	150
Chloe Austin (10)	151
Lucy-May Lewis (10)	152
George Bayles (10)	153
William Gandy (10)	154
Danielle Bromley (10)	155
Alice Jardine (10)	156
Rebecca Labdon (10)	157
Nicholas Wheadon (10)	158
Josh Nicholson (10)	159
Jessica Jeffery (10)	160
Megan Brickley (10)	161
Lee Brown (10)	162
Georgie-Anne Gray (10)	163
Ashleigh Rigden (10)	164
Chloe Burgess (10)	165
Anastasia Birch (9)	166
Emily Walker (10)	167
Ruth Bowers (10)	168
Joe Swinson (10)	169
Alice Burgess (10)	170
Samantha O'Neill (10)	171
Ryan Head (10)	172
Holly Smith (11)	173
Laurence Pellegrinelli (11)	174
Keziah Scott (11)	175
Lois Holden (9)	176
Lewis Taylor (10)	177
Sophie Farmer (9)	178
Luke Lavender (10)	179

Neroche Primary School

Jess Lawrence (9)	180
Oscar Everard (8)	181
Natalie Aicken (9)	182
Joanne Johnson (10)	183
Maria Pablo (10)	184
Jenny Kerr (9)	185
Ryan Baker (10)	186

Guy Wilson (10)   187
James Dunn (9)   188
Elizabeth Slow (10)   189
Francis Bere (10)   190
Jake Gilmore (10)   191
Zoe Smith (10)   192
Sam Lawrence (11)   193
Jodie Cox (9)   194
Lil Patuck (10)   195

St Paul's CE (VC) Junior School, Shepton Mallet

Steffi Watts (9)   196
Katie Davies (9)   197
Chloe Mason (9)   198
Ryan Burr (9)   199
Robert Wearn (9)   200
Gabriella Winter (11)   201
Joseph Ware (10)   202
Katie Green (10)   203
Georgia Short (9)   204
Samuel Bassett (9)   205
Rebecca Porter (9)   206
Lucy Chaplin (9)   207
Matthew Hatcher (9)   208
Anders Pfyl (10)   209
Lauren Hill (10)   210
Peter Key (10)   211
Sam Jones (10)   212
Kirsty Ames (10)   213
Aimée Barnstable (10)   214
Darcie Pritchard (10)   215

Wells Central CE Junior School

Jason Faulkes (10)   216
Thomas Orton (10)   217
Jay Semmler (10)   218
David Hart (10)   219

The Poems

Rain's Nice!

In some countries where it's hot,
They don't get rain quite a lot.
Except for in a monsoon,
And after that, it's bare as the moon.
I like the rain, it's nice.
It helps to grow crops, like reeds and rice.
'I think we've got too much,'
Would say my mum in a fuss.
The best thing is wearing wellies,
And looking in puddles and looking like jellies!
And I'll stay right where we are,
Actually I think I'll go home and play my guitar.
So if you ever get caught in the rain,
Just think how lucky you are
Not to be walking across the Spanish plain.

Mungo Whittingham (10)
Blackbrook Primary School

The Water Poem

The
Rain comes
tumbling down
from the sky. Everyone
needs it, I ask myself why?
We need it for baths, we need it
for drinks-drinks, we are very grateful,
and to help things grow, don't waste it
down the sink. It splishes and it splashes,
there are puddles all around, sometimes there's
a rainbow, but no treasure to be found, the water is
the treasure, take care of every bit, think as you turn the
tap on
don't
waste
another
sip!

Catherine Van-De-Burgt (10)
Blackbrook Primary School

What's The Rush?

The waves are rushing, rushing, rushing,
Slow down!
The waterfalls are gushing, gushing, gushing,
Slow down!
The tap is streaming, streaming, streaming.
Slow down!
Why can't it be dreaming, dreaming, dreaming?
Why is everything so fast?
Make things last . . .
Slow down a bit.

Emily Palmer (9)
Blackbrook Primary School

Why My Little Dolphin?

My little dolphin lives in the sea,
Why do you love me?
Why do you live in water?
You need me and I need you,
So why, why, why my little dolphin, why?

Why do you want to come for tea?
Why do you want to eat my tea?
You look like a flashing star,
Why do you look so like a raindrop?
Why my little dolphin?

Beth Harris (9)
Blackbrook Primary School

Water, Water

Water, water where do you go?
Water, water I want you.
Water, water I want you.
Water, where are you?
Water, water we need you.
Water, water we splash you.
Water, water everywhere.
Water, water are you cold?
Water, water where are you?
Water, water, raindrops to you.
Water, water everywhere!

Hannah Paddon (9)
Blackbrook Primary School

Raindrops

Raindrops falling on my head.
That's not what the weatherman said.
Jumping in puddles on my way home,
'The summer's over,' I hear my mum groan.
But I like raindrops and getting wet,
So does Billy the fish, he's my pet.
There's nothing better than wearing wellies.
Going out into the rain, getting muddy and smelly.
I jump into the bath, out come the bubbles.
Time to get daft.
'Water's fantastic,' I hear my friend laugh.

Charlie Roberts (9)
Blackbrook Primary School

Water Why?

Rain, why   fall from
                do you   the sky,
Then come down to the ground?

Why is the waterfall so rushing and gushing,
and never falling slowly like some rain?
Water, why are you always flowing in streams,
rivers and seas?
Water why are you so wavy, like some people's hair,
and never straight like my brown hair?
Water why do you come from the tap like a bouncy ball?

Water   do   never
                why   you   stop?

Rosie Crean (10)
Blackbrook Primary School

Love

Love is light red, like a heart throbbing,
It feels like flying through the sky.
It smells like a rose soaked in lavender,
It sounds like the wind running in my ear.
It tastes like melted chocolate dripping in my mouth.
It looks like the smallest bird is happy,
Love reminds me of nothing but love.

Claire Warr (10)
Blackbrook Primary School

Anger

Anger is the colour of dark red,
Anger is the colour of black,
Anger feels like a sharp pain.
Anger smells of rotten eggs,
Anger looks like lightning,
Anger tastes of mushrooms,
Anger sounds like thunder,
Anger reminds me of ghosts.

Jake Gladki (11)
Blackbrook Primary School

The Mermaid Who Never Leaves

The white horses of the sea soon fade down,
but I know someone who does not.
The seagulls fly in circles but shortly fly away,
but I know someone who does not.
The sea creatures soon die and are washed up on the beach,
but I know someone who does not.
The wonderful dolphins stay in one place
but swoop and sway away,
but I know someone who does not.
And the sea is as swivelling as a paper bag in the wind
and the sea is as twinkling as the moon, sun and stars.
So I suppose you're wondering who this person is,
well it's the sea mermaid and she's as beautiful as the most rushing
waterfall that's so bubbly in the world.
Her hair is as wavy and soft as a slithery snake wrapped in silk.
Her eyes are as colourful as a rainbow.
Her tail is as sensational as the planets and the world above.

So when you go to the seaside and if you go out deep
you will be sure to see this wonderful mermaid because she never
ever leaves!

Adrienne Hill (9)
Blackbrook Primary School

The Wonderful Mermaid

There once was a wonderful mermaid
Who had beautiful long hair
Who swam across the ocean
To the seashore fair.

She enjoyed herself very much
Then she remembered she had forgotten her water phone
She swam all the way back
And knocked on the door with a
Moan and a groan.

A big blue whale stood at the door
And asked, 'What are you looking for?'
'My phone! My phone!'
'Look over there, it's over there on the floor.'

She looked over there with complete delight,
'I had a really big fright,
Oh thank you, how can I repay you?'
'It's alright!'

Beth Delahay (9)
Blackbrook Primary School

Water

Water in the sea
Water in the pond,
Water in the river
Water in the lake.

Boats on the sea
Fishing on the pond,
Fish in the lake,
Near the river.

Michael Cole (9)
Blackbrook Primary School

Storms

S torms are amazing things
T hey're really noisy and loud
O bservant things, they make sure they make a mess
R aiding the Earth, like a stomping tiger
M um looks after my sisters as they weep
S torms are *amazing!*

Paige Burns (9)
Blackbrook Primary School

Water, Water

Water, water everywhere
Water, water has no care
Just one thing I would like to say
Where does water come from?

Water, water in your pipes
Water, water in wet wipes
Just one thing I would like to say
Where does water come from?

Water, water in the sea
Water, water doesn't bother me
Just one thing I would like to say
Where does water come from?

Water, water crashing like a thunderstorm
Water, water sometimes not very warm
Just one thing I would like to say
Where does water come from?

Water, water in the clouds
Water, water is not loud
Now I know where you come from
That's the end of that.

Natasha Stone (9)
Blackbrook Primary School

Bubbles In The Sea

The sea is blue not green or red
It's got a bit of grey in
All seas are different, none are the same
Some animals in them are quite tame.

The sea has bubbly foam in,
That fizzes and crackles all the time.
The clouds drop raindrops in the sea,
There appears a bubble once again.

Lots of creatures in the sea blow bubbles,
Just like a fish, can't you see?

Natasha Milton (9)
Blackbrook Primary School

Why Have I Got A Pond?

Why have I got a pond?
Can't I have a bench or a swing?
Why a pond?
I sit there all day,
Why a pond?

I have my bench, but I'm still wondering why a pond?
We all go outside, I'm still wondering why can't I have a sister -
Or a climbing frame?
Why a pond?

One day my friends came round and we had a party
And we all went by the pond, my dad came by and he fell in!

Now I know why I've got a pond!

Abbie Littlejohns (9)
Blackbrook Primary School

Waterfall

A waterfall was calm and clear,
but when I went up to it,
it was dirty, muddy and brown.
I went into the water to get fit.

Where does water come from?
I don't know where!
Please help me and tell me,
I know, I can go and see the mayor!

Water, water I like you,
You're nice and tasty,
Oh that's cool but one thing that I have to say is
Thank you water for a lovely day.

Charlotte Stone (9)
Blackbrook Primary School

Running Rain

Running rain, running rain, the rain just keeps running
why do you keep running rain? Why do you
disturb me? I just want to know,
just tell me please, why do you
keep me waiting? Why
do you run
from me?

Joshua Manchip (10)
Blackbrook Primary School

Water, Water

Water, water, I love water
I go swimming in water.
Water, water, I love water,
In the big blue sea, where the whale is.

Water, water, I love water
In the river where the bog is.
Water, water, I love water
In the park where the lake is.

Water, water, I love water
Where does this water come from?

Samuel Puddy (9)
Blackbrook Primary School

Waterfall

W   t   r   a   l
   a   e   f   l   Waterfall, where are you going?

W   t   r   a   l
   a   e   f   l   Waterfall, where are you going?

W   t   r   a   l
   a   e   f   l   Waterfall, keep on going?

W   t   r   a   l
   a   e   f   l   Waterfall, keep on crashing.

W   t   r   a   l
   a   e   f   l   Waterfall when do you stop?

W   t   r   a   l
   a   e   f   l   Waterfall has anyone seen you before?

W   t   r   a   l
   a   e   f   l   I love you.

Jordan Lock (9)
Blackbrook Primary School

Fear Is A Horrid Thing

Fear is as grey as a gravestone sitting
in a cemetery on its own.
It looks like a dark castle at midnight.
It sounds like a large drill digging up the road.
Fear tastes like a sour lemon.
It smells like horse dung lying
in the middle of an old street.
It feels like a knife in your head . . .
Fear reminds me of the Victorian schoolchildren.

Jordan Brooks (10)
Blackbrook Primary School

Happiness

Happiness is as pink as rosy cheeks
and as pink as flowers.
Happiness feels like a soft, velvet cushion.
Happiness smells like a pink rose,
Happiness looks like a diamond tiara.
Happiness tastes like melted chocolate.
Happiness sounds like my favourite music.
Happiness reminds me of the best times in my life.

Jessica Cook (10)
Blackbrook Primary School

Happiness

Happiness is yellow, like the sun burning in the sky,
It's hot like the sun in the sky.
It smells like a fresh daisy,
It looks like the sun in the sky with a smile on its face.
It tastes like a banana,
It sounds like a bee getting honey.
It reminds me of having fun with my friends.

Charlotte Strang (10)
Blackbrook Primary School

Happiness

Happiness is as red as a rose,
and as red as a shiny cherry too.
Happiness feels like you're on top of the world
and smells like melted chocolate.
Happiness looks like a flower that has been freshly picked,
and it tastes like a Sunday roast.
Happiness sounds like the ringing of bells
and happiness reminds me of Winnie the Pooh and
all his friends, and also how lucky in life I have been.

Lucy Cooper (10)
Blackbrook Primary School

Happiness

The colour of happiness reminds me of the wavy blue sea
Happiness smells like salty seawater.
Happiness looks like a beautiful view on top of the lovely
dark green hills.
Happiness tastes like fresh air, and trees.
The other colour of happiness is love
and it's a lovely colour to like.
It sounds like the air blowing towards me.
Happiness feels like the hot sunshine and as the
giraffes eat their leaves, it leaves all the happiness behind.

Bethany Sanders (10)
Blackbrook Primary School

Happiness

The colour of happiness is blue,
It smells like fresh cut grass.
Happiness tastes like smoothies,
It feels like a soft blanket,
Happiness sounds like blowing trees,
The colour is the sea,
Happiness reminds me of fairs and friends.

Megan Strong (10)
Blackbrook Primary School

Laughter

Laughter is like a beaming red.
It sounds like a well-played piano.
It tastes like melted chocolate,
It feels like a warm bath.
It smells like fat fried chips,
It reminds me of my team winning the league.

Jakob Pitts (10)
Blackbrook Primary School

The Upset Rabbit

The rabbit hopped to his mates,
But he couldn't reach the gate
So he yelled out loud.
Stood up tall and proud,
But still couldn't reach the gate.
So he crawled through a gap
And gave the door a tap.
Mrs Coat opened the door
The rabbit asked for Paul.
But Mrs Coat smiled at him,
And said, 'Sorry, he's not in!'
So the rabbit went home upset.

Laura Orton (11)
Blackbrook Primary School

Love

Love is pink like a heart,
It feels like the sun shining on you.
It smells like a summer's breeze,
It sounds like a flowing river,
Twisting this way and that.
It tastes like a night on the sea,
It looks like the rural countryside.
It reminds me of a rose swaying in the breeze.

Declan Heaslewood (10)
Blackbrook Primary School

Happiness

Happiness is the colour yellow, like a daffodil
It feels like the sun shining
It smells like a roast, cooking in the kitchen
It sounds like my favourite music playing
It tastes like melted chocolate
It looks like a flower which is growing
It reminds me of my sister and brothers.

Samantha Oaten (10)
Blackbrook Primary School

Love Is . . .

Love is the calmest light blue in the world,
as calm as the sea.
Love feels like you're about to burst
with sweetness and kindness.
Love smells like a box of white chocolates and flowers,
all colours of the rainbow.
Love sounds like a happy couple sitting at a table for two
at a posh restaurant.
Love tastes like a tub of strawberry ice cream.
Love looks like a beautiful red rose.
Love reminds me of two doves, sitting together.

Lauren Hull (10)
Blackbrook Primary School

Love

Love is pink hearts,
Love is full of arts.
Love is so beautiful,
Love is so colourful.
Love is full of power,
Love is the smell of a flower.
Love is amazing,
Love is classical music, fading.

Katherine Cross (10)
Blackbrook Primary School

Love

Love is the colour of pink
        for the love and the kisses.
Love is the colour of pink
        for the pink primroses, sugar plum princess
        and chocolate, while Mum's giving me kisses.
Love feels like a little bit of your
        tummy is filled with happiness.
Love smells like pink roses
        just blooming, the honey just being opened.
Love sounds like a puppy
        crying for its mummy.
Love tastes like your mum's perfume
        in your mouth, urgh!
Love looks like me and my mum
        hugging and kissing.
Love reminds me of the happiness
        of my family.

Kimberley Butler (10)
Blackbrook Primary School

Happiness

Happiness is a yellow and goldy colour
Like a star in the sky

Happiness feels like a smile inside
It smells like roses

Happiness sounds like chicks tweeting
It tastes like a nice cool ice cream

Happiness looks like the sunrise
It reminds me of sunbathing.

Tom Dennett (10)
Blackbrook Primary School

Love

Love is the colour of pink
like a pink fluffy pillow
Love is the colour of pink
like a lovely pink heart
Love feels like a rumbling sound
like if you go on a blind date
Love smells like a hot dinner
like someone cooked a romantic tea
Love sounds like beautiful singing
on Valentine's Day
Love tastes like sweets
of all different flavours
Love looks like different flowers
in all different colours
Love reminds me of a wedding
with a bride and groom.

Jessica Stone (10)
Blackbrook Primary School

Darkness

Darkness is as black as the night,
Darkness sounds like the whistling wind.
Darkness smells like an abandoned, collapsed cave.
Darkness looks like a shadow covering the Earth in its slumber.
Darkness feels like ice.
Darkness tastes like ice cubes.
Darkness reminds me of a stone, covering the planet in shadows.

Daniel Cole (10)
Blackbrook Primary School

A Tear Of Sadness

The colour of it is blue, like the sky.
It sounds like a cool breeze on a hot day.
It tastes like salt.
It looks like rain falling from the sky.
It smells like you.
It feels like something cold and wet
dripping down your face.
It reminds me of the clear blue sea, glittering
as it smashes to the ground and splashes,
leaving a little puddle on that spot.

Tshana Trivella (10)
Blackbrook Primary School

Darkness

Darkness is black, like the night sky,
It feels like cold air.
It looks like a mouldy muffin.
It tastes like mushrooms.
It sounds like the crickets when they rub their legs.
It reminds me of the Devil.

Callum Hardy (10)
Blackbrook Primary School

Happiness

Happiness is a bright yellow,
Happiness reminds me of the sun.
Happiness tastes like chocolate.
Happiness is seeing my mum,
Happiness smells like flowers.
Happiness sounds like a triangle, *ting ting!*

Shannon Toop (10)
Blackbrook Primary School

Laying In The Dark One Day

Laying in the dark one day
I heard the TV blaring,
Like a teacher that had just called, 'Quiet!'
But the children were past caring.

Laying in the dark one day,
I heard a car's engine purring,
I knew it wouldn't get far
Because a splutter kept occurring.

Laying in the dark one day
I heard a door creaking,
I felt like I was in a cage
With a mouse that wouldn't stop squeaking.

Laying in the dark one day
I heard a plane go over my head,
It made me think of World War II
And all the people that are dead.

Laying in the dark one day
I heard voices in my home
My brother talking like a radio
And my mum on the phone.

Laying in the dark one day
I heard a door bang like a drum,
Next I thought I heard a trumpet
As if a marching band, had come.

Lucy O'Shea (10)
Blackbrook Primary School

Happiness

The colour of happiness is yellow
like the blazing sun,
Orange is like happiness too,
like a burning fire.
It feels like bouncing on a
bouncy castle.
It smells like freshly cut grass.
It looks like a big yellow sunflower.
It tastes like a chocolate cake.
It sounds like happy shouting children.
It reminds me of my birthday at Woodlands.

Luke Baker (10)
Blackbrook Primary School

Where Does All The Water Go?

When it rains, the next day
It always goes to waste.
So tell me in haste,
Just in case I don't know
When I'm older . . .
Where does all the water go?

Hannah Daniel (9)
Blackbrook Primary School

The White Sea Horse

Beautiful horse
Blossom's her name.
The sun rising like a fire burning in the sky.
That's what makes the sea, orange and beige.
She goes in her cave, sitting like a queen.
The royal horse always screams.
Beautiful horse.
Blossom's her name.
Amazing white coat, shiny and grey.
She opens the heavens with her black hooves.
Blossom sits on her stone
Saying, 'Gather, gather, sea friends.'

Chloe Oaten (9)
Blackbrook Primary School

Sea Monkey

There once was a monkey
Who fell in the sea.
He was wet and hungry, like me before tea.
He was all shivery.
Like a man with brain freeze.
So I asked him how he was.
He said, 'Like a man on a big grey horse.'
I forced him to swim with me in the deep blue sea.

He said, 'No, it's too cold for me.'
So I pulled him in.
I taught him to swim and
We spent all day, swimming away.
That's all I can say.

Matthew O'Shea (9)
Blackbrook Primary School

The Wonderful Waterfall

There was a waterfall
All high and rushing
The big rocks are sharp
The water's always gushing.

The water at the bottom, is very deep
A little fish fell down the waterfall
The little fish swam away
Over the top of the waterfall, you can see
The sun rise and night fall.

The water slows down as sunset falls
I jump in the water at the bottom
And I swim like a fish
I wrap myself in a towel as smooth
As cotton.

I jump into the tent and fall asleep
I heard an owl hooting, so it seems
The water started to bubble and get hotter
And hotter
I wake up the next morning -
It was all a dream!

Jessica Scott (9)
Blackbrook Primary School

Midnight Foxes

A snowy night drifts through the garden,
Midnight chimes from the church clock,
Willow fox awakes.

The moon sparkles over his amber body,
He glides through the forest
Over a wall, a meadow he finds.

He hears a shot,
In a dapple of moonlight.
He sees a scarlet trickle running down his back,
He falls
He is dead!

Laura Sandford (9)
Charlton Mackrell CE Primary School

The Charcoal Face

It was a humid day
When I saw the charcoal face.
His face was weird,
He had a beard.
It was black and white
He looked as if he could win a fight.
Then he came alive,
Went to the pool and did a dive.
I followed him in
But Mum had already thrown him in the bin!

Marcus Pile (9)
Charlton Mackrell CE Primary School

The Willow Man

As the willow man came to life,
He sprinted down the M5.
Edging towards the woods
The willow man was out of sight.
Dodging in and out the trees
Jumping over the logs,
With his flexible arms and legs,
He cartwheeled out!

Next, he got on the bus
Heading towards the town,
He read a sign, *London*
Happy he was at the time,
Climbing up Big Ben,
Scared he was, first time.
Suddenly he jumped off,
He was flying through the air,
Landed on his well-weaved legs.

Oliver Alexander (9)
Charlton Mackrell CE Primary School

Out Of Willow

Bending
Flexing,
Twisting
Whizzing,
Nothing at all emerged.

Tiring
Singing,
Staggering
Wringing,
Nothing at all emerged.

We . . .
Weaved in and out,
Round about,
An image began to emerge.

We . . .
Built it up,
To a fox pup,
An animal had emerged.

Although we were tired,
We had to admire
Our lovely handiwork.

Yasmin India Wolfe (8)
Charlton Mackrell CE Primary School

The Charcoal Face

The picture sits in its frame,
Those gleaming eyes and golden teeth!
Its evil look and sharp horns,
The hairy beard and pale cheeks.
The horrid eyes always on me,
The long nose and wide mouth.
I want to run, but I can't!
I'm sucked into the frame,
And I see the man walking past me, grinning.

Tristan Goldsmid (9)
Charlton Mackrell CE Primary School

A Willow Vixen

A willow vixen awakens -
It's a dark glittery night.
In amazing light,
Her coat turns to rich brown.

It rains,
Thunders,
Never stops!

She hunts for rabbits
Her nose pointing
At the musty smell.
In amazing light.

Charlotte-Clare Wisniewski (8)
Charlton Mackrell CE Primary School

The Charcoal Face

One night when the moon was bright
I was in the classroom and I had a fright,
A charcoal face had come alive
And was staring at me with his big, angry eyes.
I ran to the door and shoved
And shoved but it wouldn't budge.

The charcoal face screamed at me
To try and take it out of its frame.
I screamed back at it, *'No! No!'*
But a hand came out and pulled me closer.
I pushed and pulled with all my might
But the charcoal hand was too tight.

Charlotte Jane Male (9)
Charlton Mackrell CE Primary School

The Willow Man

The willow man
With the grubby hands
Wove round the frame
He had a fab aim.

Speedily he wove and groaned
While the school was phoned

The willow man
Thought hard and deep
He wanted to catch a wink of sleep

The police charged in
And arrested him
So he suffered in jail
And turned very pale
That poor old willow man.

Sophie Baker (10)
Charlton Mackrell CE Primary School

Charcoal Face

One cold night when the moon was shining,
I heard a voice of someone whining.
I looked below through a dark, cold well,
And saw a little dark-haired girl.

I turned around to get some help,
It was then when I saw the charcoal face.
I fainted and fell
Straight into the well and the little girl caught me.

She said, 'Hello, what's your name?'
But I didn't say, I was too afraid.
I opened my eyes and got a fright,
Then I looked and saw a bright, bright light.

I saw the girl with one of her mates,
But I knew it wasn't a human face.
I stood up on the ground of the well,
Then I screamed and screamed until my face swelled.

Abigail Jane Smart (9)
Charlton Mackrell CE Primary School

The Willow Foxes

Sturdy and still stands a sleeping creature,
The church bell ticks.
With a sudden jolt the ground shivers.
Ding! Dong! It's midnight!

In the garden, the willow foxes come out to play.
Down shines the moon with silver beams of light,
Upon the foxes' playground.

The foxes give a sudden leap, with a heap of joy
Over the wall.

A moonlit field shows their true colour, rusty brown.

The living beasts stalk an innocent rabbit to fill their hunger,
Sated, they skip through the dark forest, home.

As dawn breaks, they settle to sleep,
Until they wake again.

Alice Achard (10)
Charlton Mackrell CE Primary School

The Willow Fox

He lives in my shed,
The willow fox.
He climbs in
And sits in the cat box.
At night
In the moonlight,
He jumps out and
Runs about
And chases my cat.
Fancy that!
Then he
Leaps back inside.

The willow fox.

Sean Webster (9)
Charlton Mackrell CE Primary School

The Willow Foxes

In the night, stars twinkle,
A shooting star shoots over the foxes.
The clock stops; they come alive.
Bushy tails glitter in the moonlight.
Their beady eyes light up,
As they pounce into the mist,
They return the morning after.

Samantha Lucy Churcher (10)
Charlton Mackrell CE Primary School

Willow Fox

There it was, a sparkling gingerish fox,
Who once woke up to real life!
As a big cloud of thick fog hovered over
Charlton Mackrell church,
He, the fox, rose
And as he flew, sparkling, to the top of the hill,
He saw the dazzling school.

Nathan Harris (9)
Charlton Mackrell CE Primary School

The Birds And Tabby

The birds in our garden
Play and sing all day,
They are mostly timid in their own sort of way.
Through the tree, they dart,
They swoop from the tree and
On the bough, they nest.

All snug and cosy through the night,
They keep their eggs warm with pure delight.

Then a midnight prowler, tabby cat drops by,
For a snack he comes,
With a pounce and a leap
Tabby drops back to the ground.
Tabby cries hungrily, tears in his eyes,
With a stealthy jump into the tree,
Gently tabby sobs,
No birds left at all!
With a jump he's out of the tree,
Briskly he trundles away, without a trace.

That wasn't the last of tabby we've seen,
That wasn't the last of tabby, we've seen!

Catherine May Baynes (9)
Charlton Mackrell CE Primary School

Willow Fox

Night falls
Fox awakens!
He guards the stone school,
Proudly prowling.
Muscular clockwork feet,
Spring into the field.
Ripping turf in his claws
As he pounces on a rabbit.
He howls to the luminous moon
And bounds back
To the motionless garden.

Mitchel William Newbury (10)
Charlton Mackrell CE Primary School

The Willow Man

The willow man is coming,
The willow man is marching.
Over the hill, snapping, bending,
Breaking, staggering
Over the moor.
The willow man is coming!

Michael James Male (11)
Charlton Mackrell CE Primary School

The Willow Fox

When the willow fox goes out at midnight,
It leaps into the fox hole.
In the beautiful night, the weather's clear.
The willow fox is so real.
The fox, flying through the night,
Willow fox hunting in the night.
The night fox stalking in the night.
And the willow fox suddenly turns real in the night.

Jonathan Girt (9)
Charlton Mackrell CE Primary School

Doughnut

Delicious jam doughnut
Only for me!
Up it comes! I bite,
Giggling always,
Hiding behind it,
Nice and jammy.
Up to my mouth -
Too yummy to share!

Kirsti Rendall (8)
Charlton Mackrell CE Primary School

Charcoal Face

We rubbed, we scrubbed,
We scribbled, we dribbled,
And out of it came a charcoal face!
It was fun, it was exciting,
And we did it all day long.
The face was white, the face was black,
The face was every colour in mind.

Lee Parsons (10)
Charlton Mackrell CE Primary School

The Willow Fox

One dark night, the willow fox awoke
Then it was gone
Flown away through the trees
Chasing a willow duck
Up to the sparkly stars
In the morning it was still too
Dark to touch.

Josh Rydon (9)
Charlton Mackrell CE Primary School

The Fox

Foxy, Foxy, coat of red
Chasing chickens in the shed,
In the evening, eyes a-glowing
Mr Fox knows where he's going.

Suburban animal he's become
Has no fear of anyone,
Not afraid to be seen
As he lets out a lonely scream.

Cunning fox, his eyes so bright,
He goes prowling all the night.
Only stopping by and by,
Ears pricking at a vixen's cry.

Katy Aldridge (9)
Chilthorne Domer Church School

The Dolphin

Dancing so graceful up and down the waves,
Gliding fast in the salty sea
Jumping through the wiggly spray,
Backflip through the breezy air
In the midday sky
Looping backwards and forwards
Jumping and catching fish.

Cassandra Broadbent (10)
Chilthorne Domer Church School

The Otter

Otter, otter, glide away
Otter, otter, go and play.
Otter, otter, dive down deep,
Otter, otter, hide and peep.

Otter, otter, float around,
Otter, otter, touch the ground.
Otter, otter, swim to shore
He'll eat fish for evermore.

Jessica Baker (9)
Chilthorne Domer Church School

Tiger

Tiger hiding in the grass,
Sneaking to his prey,
Crouching, staring,
Ready to jump.

Prowling through the grass,
Leaping in the air,
Pouncing but missing.

Chasing through grass
Tearing his prey,
Then only silence!

Timothy Batstone (9)
Chilthorne Domer Church School

The Otter

Otter, otter, in the river
Flowing fast, saw a silver glimpse go past.

Otter, otter, diving deep down
Into the waters brown
Grasping the fish, he has found.

Then swimming on without a sound,
The king of the river -
Without a crown.

Elise Burt (9)
Chilthorne Domer Church School

The Penguin

The penguin dives
Into the cold, icy sea,
Driving upwards
And gliding within the waves.
Being lifted,
Hearing nothing but crash after crash,
Magnified by the icy cliffs off a frozen beach.
Flowing with the cool spray,
The waves
Calm down.
It rises with the wind and sea,
Rising and descending.
It swims along,
Looking at fish in the freezing deep.
Diving deep
Into salty sea.
Backflip
Twisting and turning in the waves.
Catching a fish before it
Climbs the waves
And eats its prey.
Landing on a floating iceberg
And diving off again.

Jasmine Burton (10)
Chilthorne Domer Church School

The Snake

Slithering slowly out of the rock
Wriggling through the log.
He sees his prey struggling
He creeps up slowly
Then eats him, violently.

He zooms back to his house
And slithers back into his black dark tree
Then goes to sleep.

Jessica Bushell (10)
Chilthorne Domer Church School

Kitten

Kitten! Kitten! Small and sweet,
She has little furry feet.
Watch her sleep, night and day
Using a bed full of hay.

Milk is her favourite treat,
Bottle-fed with a teat!
In my mummy cat peeps.
Hear me purr and watch me leap!

Jemma Callow (9)
Chilthorne Domer Church School

The Golden Eagle

Golden eagle flying around
Swooping on its prey
Eating on a rock.

Diving in the water
Coming out with
A big fish in his beak.

Gliding to his home,
Feeding his young.

Ryan Coombes (10)
Chilthorne Domer Church School

The Lion

Lion, lion, catching prey,
In the night-time he does lay
Scratching something with his paw
To feast and to have a roar.

Creeping round to the jungle beat
Creating it with his big feet.
Catching zebras with his big claws
Then crunching bones with his jaws.

At night-time he goes back home
Nowhere else to go and roam
In his cave, he has a peep
Then he settles down to sleep.

Jade Frost (10)
Chilthorne Domer Church School

The Otter

Otter, otter plays around,
Otter, otter floating round.
Otter, otter, slide away
Otter, otter, play all day.

Otter, otter, glide to shore,
Otter otter, dive down deep, to the floor.
Otter, otter, swim, swim, swim,
Otter, otter look at him.

Chloe Giles (9)
Chilthorne Domer Church School

Kitten

Kitten! Kitten! Curled up tight,
In the middle of the night.
Mother cat is just nearby,
Keeping out a watchful eye.

Kitten! Kitten! Wake up quick,
Mother says she wants to lick,
Morning time, a bright new day,
All kitten wants to do is play.

Kitten! Kitten! Plays with wool,
Throws it up, now that's real cool!
Watch out mouse, he's spotted you,
Mouse runs off, now who's the fool?

Kitten! Kitten! Wants to sleep,
Tired eyes just want to peep.
Mother says, 'It's time for bed,
So lie down and rest your head.'

Georgia Green (9)
Chilthorne Domer Church School

Monkey

Monkey, monkey, zooming round
Fell over and hit the ground
Ouch! He broke his leg
Oh no! Here's his mum
Oooh! She kicked him up the bum!

Monkey, monkey, he wet himself
Then he went into a stealth
He's so mad he joined the navy
But all the beds are full of gravy.

Monkey, monkey, swinging on trees
He fell and grazed his knees.
On his first day he said, *'Wow!'*
And a cat said, 'Miaow!'

Aaron Baker (10)
Chilthorne Domer Church School

The Tiger

An orange and black flash
Running as fast as the wind
Staring bright eyes
Straight ahead at his prey.
Jumping, fiercely attacking
Killing, gnawing
Then silently, dragging
His dinner
In his enormous jaws
Alone to enjoy
His delicious feast.

Jordon Higgins (9)
Chilthorne Domer Church School

Monkey

Spinning on his pole
Running for his prey,
Gliding on the water.
Swimming in the pool,
Swinging from the trees,
Making monkey noises.
Panting hard,
Jumping overhead,
Sprinting home.

Rebecca Pearce (9) & Taela Horrigan (10)
Chilthorne Domer Church School

Monkey

Monkey, monkey, swinging by
In the treetops, very high
Monkey, monkey, sitting in the trees
Eating bananas all day long.

Monkey, monkey, looking at me
What have you got in your tree?
Monkey, monkey, staring at me
Will you share your bananas with me?

Megan Johnson (9)
Chilthorne Domer Church School

Monkey

Monkey swinging from his perch
Somersaulting to grab a next vine.
Running down enormous steep cliffs,
Jumping over invisible spikes,
Zigzagging through gigantic roots
Leaping onto the next vine,
Zooming to his goal.

Adam Webber (9)
Chilthorne Domer Church School

The Badger

Badger, badger, black and white
My dad sees them every night,
Badger has a stripy nose
In and out the sett he goes.

Badger, badger hunting round
With his nose close to the ground,
Slugs and snails will be found
Making his snuffling sound.

Badger, badger, black and white
My dad sees them every night,
Badger has a stripy nose
In and out the sett he goes.

Jack Sharp (10)
Chilthorne Domer Church School

The Otter

Otter, otter, swimming fast,
With a fish in his clasp
Munching, chewing, a tasty treat
Kicking fast with his feet.

In deep water with a friend,
Gosh this fun will never end.
Swimming fast, come now please
You can catch me with great ease.

This race is tough,
But I'm in the lead,
I'll glide ahead
And win with greed.
Hooray! Hooray! I have won
I'll take my prize and then I'll run!

Liam Parsons (10)
Chilthorne Domer Church School

The Otter

Otter! Otter! Swimming champ.
In his mouth, a fish he clamps.
A family at home awaits!
He doesn't want to be late!

The lake starts to get dark.
But it still seems like a park!
Otters slide here and there.
Still playing like bears!

Lloyd Kannair & Leon Mahoney (10)
Chilthorne Domer Church School

The Monkey

Monkey, monkey in the trees,
Eating bananas as it pleases,
Swinging through the trees with ease,
Playing hide the hunter's keys.

Up the tallest tree you'll find,
Only if you're very kind,
Monkeys look and then they smile,
At the mother of this child.

The newborn baby child has grown,
Now there is no need to moan,
For it can now chatter away,
It is never a quiet day.

Monkey, monkey in the trees,
Eating bananas as it pleases,
Swinging through the trees with ease,
Bye-bye to the hunter's keys,
Splash!

Natasha Jones (10)
Chilthorne Domer Church School

The Dolphin

Dolphin, dolphin splashing around,
Making such a squeaky sound,
Diving up and down the waves,
Swimming with friends to the caves.

Munching on fish for their tea,
Swimming through the seven seas,
Playing with you friends all day,
Playing in the frothy spray.

Dolphin, dolphin splashing around,
Making such a squeaky sound,
Goodbye dolphin, swim away,
Come and play another day.

Megan Knight (10)
Chilthorne Domer Church School

The Hippo

Hippo, hippo walking slow,
On the riverbed below.
How you wallow in the deep,
There you swim and there you sleep.

Your skin so smooth, all around,
Those small legs keep you off the ground.
Your large head and tiny ears,
Open mouth fills us with fear.

You lie so still, like a rock,
Closely watching, taking stock.
Huge jaws crashing as you fight,
Yet so gentle, are we right?

Hippo, hippo walking slow,
On the riverbed below.
How you wallow in the deep,
There your secrets you will keep.

Jessica Ogden (10)
Chilthorne Domer Church School

The Lion

Lion, lion, prowling round,
Making a loud growling sound,
The lion crawls through the plain,
Eating everything he'd gain.

Who could build your fearful form?
Who made your rough mane so torn?
Creeping round to a jungle beat,
Who created your big feet?

Who made your bushy brown tail?
You catch a deer, you can't fail,
Who could make your paws so tough?
Who is making you play rough?

Lion, lion, running round,
Making a loud growling sound,
Then he crawls through the plain,
Eating everything he'd gain.

Amy Wroot (10)
Chilthorne Domer Church School

The Dolphin

Dolphin, dolphin in the sea,
How you fill my heart with glee,
Splishing, splashing, jumping high,
Acrobatics in the sky.

Dolphin, dolphin how I wish,
That I was a graceful fish,
How my heart would fill with pride,
Swimming with you, side by side.

Tia Shrimpton (9)
Chilthorne Domer Church School

My Brother

My little brother,
Has got very curly hair.
He always cuddles his teddy bear.
He is three years old,
And very bold.
My brother is good,
And gets in my hood.
He gives me hugs,
Pulls and tugs.
    I love my brother,
    He is so cute.

Hannah Derrick (8)
Curry Mallet CE Primary School

Preparing For War

Soldiers lining up in platoons,
Checking their rifles so they don't go boom,
Tank commanders sitting up top,
People saying, 'Stop, stop, stop!'
Radars beeping, radios buzzing,
Planes chugging,
People running.

During war, people die,
And with that others scream, 'Why?'
Machine guns firing, *boom, boom, boom,*
Tank shells hitting, then *kaboom*.

Alex Manu (10)
Curry Mallet CE Primary School

Fire

The fire crackled, burning softly,
Sparks flew,
Swooping and diving like swallows in the wind.

The fire reached up, licking the air,
Tasting like a tongue,
Twisting and turning like a worm.

The fire crackled,
Talking lazily to the breeze,
Air lapping over it like crashing waves.

The fire burned onwards,
Crying embers,
Slowly dying into nothingness.

Sam Murray (10)
Curry Mallet CE Primary School

What I'm Going To Be

I don't know what I'm going to be when I grow up,
I could try selling my mum's best cup,
But there again we've already sold it,
So we have the money to keep Dad fit,
I could worship and be a nun,
After all it would be much more fun,
I'd play tennis in the garden,
I'd never go to kindergarten,
I'd never leave the abbey walls,
Else I would have a big downfall,
I'd go and see the abbey mother,
I'd be in a big spot of bother,
Yes, I think I'll be a nun,
After all it would be much more fun,
Than looking after a baby fawn,
Or mowing the grass of a big, green lawn.

Zoë Sanders (8)
Curry Mallet CE Primary School

My Football

On Saturday I go to different places to play football
We play half-pitch
And our kit is gold and blue.

The ref gives fouls, throw-ins and corners too
We'd better not make a bad tackle
Or the ref will blow for a foul.

We have always got to score to win.

We've all got favourite players
Some of mine are Beckham, Ronaldo and Nistlerooy
I also like Rooney, Scholes and Smith.

My football is great!

Brandon Payn (8)
Curry Mallet CE Primary School

Horse Breeds

From the golden dazzling Palomino,
To the spotted American Appaloosa,

The little tough Scottish Highland,
Or the flashy grey Lipizzanner,

Now on to the showjumping Selle Française,
And the stocky Shetland,

The strong, tall Shire,
To the Old English Fell,

From the competition Swedish Warmblood,
To the dressage French Anglo-Arab,

The Clydesdale, powerful, used to heavy work,
And all Arabians, full of energy and stamina,

Now on to the Friesian, black and dramatic,
The mini Falabella, small but complete,

The Dales pony, vigorous and secure,
And the New Forest, always reliable,

Finally on to the solid Connemara,
Not forgetting a driving type, the Gelderlander.

Ella Sanders (11)
Curry Mallet CE Primary School

Cats

My cats are naughty,
My cats are cuddly,
My cats are really small.
They run really fast,
They have long, smooth tails,
They cry loud and squeaky.

They are sneaky,
They are soft,
They get really hungry.
My cats have incredibly small ears,
My cats are really playful,
My cats have thin, long legs.

My cats are sometimes fluffy,
My cats are sometimes fat,
My cats have sharp, pointy claws.
They are sometimes messy,
They are always sleepy,
They are amazingly funny.

Larissa Charlesworth (10)
Curry Mallet CE Primary School

Midnight Magic

Crash went the window
As a bird splats on the pane
Oh I do so hope it will never happen again
I pulled the string to open the blind
I looked out the window and thought I'd lost my mind
It wasn't a bird at all
It was a horse, elegant and tall
But there was something peculiar about this stallion
It had wings as white as a polar bear's talon
He took me to the moon
And said, 'We'll be home soon.'
I saw his friend
It was a monster, it wasn't pretend
Then he took me to his land
We had to cross a bridge as thin as a hair strand
I met his mum, she filled my tum
With a delicious gooey gum
'I'm really tired, I want to go home.'
'OK,' he said, in a soothing tone
I went to bed with my cuddly ted
In the morning, Uncle came
Panting and looking boiling
He had a present, for me of course
It was a winged, white horse
It looked like the one I did ride
He had a glint in his eye
Then I'm sure I saw him smile.

Maisy Bond (9)
Curry Mallet CE Primary School

Dogs

Dogs are loving, cuddly, smelly, small
Soft, furry, fat, noisy and tall
Some with rough fur, some with smooth
Some dogs have fluffy ears, some smoothed-haired
Dogs have long tongues to lick up their dinner
Some on a diet to get them thinner
Old dogs - slow, young dogs - fast
Memorable days of the past
Dogs get tired and floppy
At the end of the day, making them soppy.

Molly Welch (10)
Curry Mallet CE Primary School

Battle

Big Chinooks going into battle,
The two blades begin to rattle,
The gunners get ready to shoot,
And then we see a flying boot,
A pilot starts to choke,
As I see a puff of smoke,
I jump on the gun,
And I start to have fun.
The enemy died,
It looked like they did not try.

Michael Albrow (9)
Curry Mallet CE Primary School

Snow

Fluffy snow gently drifts out of the sky
Children coming out to play
With their coats, scarves, gloves and boots
Making snowmen and snow fights
Wet and cold, must warm up
Get a hot chocolate
That will warm you up.

Esme Hebditch (9)
Curry Mallet CE Primary School

All Year Round

Winter whips round
With snow and wind
It's cold and bitter
With frosted rings

Spring with daffodils
And light showers
A bit of sun too

Summer sun
Hot, yellow days
Swimming and
Tennis, cricket too

Brown and orange
Yellow and green
Leaves are falling
On top of me.

Harriet Roberts (9)
Curry Mallet CE Primary School

The Match

The players came onto the pitch,
Their boots muddy already,
The ref blows his whistle for kick-off,
And the game begins.

They kick the ball,
And it flies far,
The goalie catches it,
And gives it a kick.

I try to volley it and I do,
It misses and frustration comes to me,
The goalie kicks it,
And I get the ball.

I dribble it down the wet, wet pitch,
A player slides me down,
'Free kick,' cries the ref,
And I take the kick.

It goes in the goal,
And I cry, 'Yes.'
The players hug me,
And the ref blows his whistle.

'One-nil,' the ref shouts,
We all celebrate,
The team go off,
And we get the trophy.

Oliver Lucas (9)
Curry Mallet CE Primary School

Football

Scoring goals is really fun,
Slowly falling to the ground,
Zooming fast into the net,
Red and yellow cards we get,
'Goal!' I shout, the goalie falls,
The clapping sounds like a thunderstorm,
Tackling boys is oh so cool,
So is England winning the World Cup.

Jenna Sparks (9)
Curry Mallet CE Primary School

Spooky

Spooky house
Little mouse
Sitting in the corner.

Spooky ghost
Scaring the host
Down the corridor.

Looking at the grave
Known by Dave
In the spooky graveyard.

I see a stalker
Killing my daughter
Entering the doorway.

Harry Dibble (9)
Curry Mallet CE Primary School

Christmas Poem

C arols being sung in church,
H appy people playing in the snow,
R hymes being sung by gorgeous angels,
I love Christmas ever so much,
S anta Claus is coming to town,
T rees covered in sparkly baubles,
M agical Santa cheering up children,
A shiny star on top of the tree,
S nowmen being constructed.

Sophia Eminson (9)
Curry Mallet CE Primary School

Clouds

When I look at the clouds I see
   an eagle swooping for its prey.

When I look at the clouds I see
   a crocodile grinning, horrible to see.

When I look at the clouds I see
   a yummy sweet waiting for me.

When I look at the clouds I see
   a heart just waiting for a friend.

Kya Robson (9)
Curry Mallet CE Primary School

Stars

Shooting stars all year round
And they never touch the ground
They are white
And you won't know their height
They're shining at night
And when it's dark in the morning.

Ebony Cossey (9)
Curry Mallet CE Primary School

The Farrier

Furnaces are hot, heating the horseshoes
Bellows puffing hard, making the fire roar
Horseshoes are made out of iron
Nailed to the horses' feet
A smithy can earn lots of money.

David Troutt (9)
Curry Mallet CE Primary School

Clouds

When I look at the clouds I see . . .
A bat swooping towards me
A rhino charging at a tree
Maybe a UFO falling into the sea
Sometimes a tank blasting a quay.

Dominic Slade (9)
Curry Mallet CE Primary School

Landini Tractor

Landini is a wrestler who can knock you flat,
Landini is a weightlifter who can lift 100 tons,
Landini is a lion with a really ferocious roar,
Landini is a remote control car with loads of levers.
Landini is a mountain many times taller than me,
Landini is a horse cantering through the fields.

Daisy Baggs (10)
Kingsbury Episcopi Primary School

Shark Is

A shark is a cheetah in the water, fast and deadly.
It is a gun, killing seals.
It is the king of the sea, proud and in command.
It is a giant mouth, filled with razor-sharp teeth.
It is a warrior, armed with a shield and sword.

Josh Smith (10)
Kingsbury Episcopi Primary School

Tiger

Her claws are razors, sharp and dangerous.
Her teeth are daggers, ready to stab.
Her eyes are diamonds, twinkling in the night.
She is a taxi zooming past.
She's fire flickering at night.
She's thunder roaring.
I'm counting her steps
Watch out she's . . .
. . . *close*

Grace Green (10)
Kingsbury Episcopi Primary School

Thunder And Lightning

Lightning is a torch lighting up the room.
Thunder is like saucepans in the sky rumbling noisily.
Lightning is a gold medal winner of the sprint race.
Thunder is a storm-warning over the radio.
Lightning is a giant's light bulb at the disco.
Thunder is a warrior fighting battles in the sky.

Brad Cole (10)
Kingsbury Episcopi Primary School

A Tiger Is

He is a dark fox, sneaky and cunning.
A missile, streamlined and fast, hunting alongside his shadow.
A sprinter on the athletic track, fast and furious.
He is a hound dog tracking his prey,
Stalking the grasslands for a sign of life.
He is a hare leaping on his prey.

Daniel Brain (11)
Kingsbury Episcopi Primary School

Buzzard

He is a brown dart, zooming through the air.
He is a flashing piece of gold, hitting the ground.
He is a streak of lightning in the sky.
He is a rock, hard and sharp.
He is a fast car, squealing through the air.
He is a dangerous roundabout, circling his prey.
He is a brown aeroplane, spinning in the clouds.

Jacob Ralph (9)
Kingsbury Episcopi Primary School

A Cheetah Is

He is lightning fast!
He is an eagle, a super-swift predator.
He is a stalker in the long grass, after his prey.
He is a T-rex, fierce when catching his prey.
He is pyjamas, soft and warm.
He is a big, spotty teddy bear.

Tom Moore (10)
Kingsbury Episcopi Primary School

Lightning

Lightning is a light bulb blowing out.
It is a yellow pencil, drawing across a dark sky.
It is a shooting star high up in space.
It is a broken electric cable, giving off sparks.
It is a shiny piece of metal reflecting itself.

Callum Corbett (10)
Kingsbury Episcopi Primary School

Horse

It is a rocket, galloping across the fields.
It can be a frog, jumping high over fences.
It is a gust of wind, bucking and rearing.
It is a taxi, taking me where I want to go.
It is a friend, someone to talk to.

Ieshia Rashbrook (9)
Kingsbury Episcopi Primary School

Book

A book is action, waiting to happen in your mind.
It is a time line with chapters of time.
It is an adventure in a made-up world.
It is a pool of words.
It is an unknown world.
It is a world of characters.

Alice Miller (9)
Kingsbury Episcopi Primary School

Tiger

She's an orange taxi rushing past.
She's thunder roaring in the night.
She's a giant kitten with bright stripes.
Her claws are razors.
Her teeth are daggers.
Her nose is a wet sponge.
Her eyes are bright beads.
She's lightning zooming away . . .
I wonder where?

Honor Elliott (10)
Kingsbury Episcopi Primary School

What Is A Tiger

A tiger is a rough jacket with stripes of leather.
She is a worn-away sheepskin rug.
She is music so loud, it hurts your ears.
She is blood dripping into a drain after a kill.
She is a huge lake rippling in the sun.
A tiger is a tree house waiting to be found.

Briannie Faull (10)
Kingsbury Episcopi Primary School

Shark Is

A shark is a hunter looking for his prey.
His teeth are pencils, snapped and jagged.
His is a cheetah bursting forward towards his meal.
Her is a kitchen extractor, filtering the steam.
His mouth is a gaping hole, ready to bite.

Chris Glyde (10)
Kingsbury Episcopi Primary School

The Gold Cat

He is a knight in shining armour, so brave.
He is a gust of wind, so fast.
His eyes are like street lamps, so bright.
His hairs are static electricity, when he is running by.
He is a hot-water bottle in the morning, lying on my bed.
He is a really good hunter seeking his prey.
He is a golden streak of colour in the dark.

Charlotte Gilliam (10)
Kingsbury Episcopi Primary School

Rain

It is a water pistol on a hot day.
It is a puddle, kicked all over me.
It is a water balloon, bursting and covering me
and my friends.
It is a low cloud, misty and damp.
It is a shower for a bird in a tree.
It is the spray from a wave, crashing against a cliff.

Sam Reed (9)
Kingsbury Episcopi Primary School

Stream

A stream is a gently flowing tap.
It is a pebbly beach.
It is a swimming pool on a hot day.
It is a slide of water.
It is a smooth pebble.
It is a trickling water feature.
It is a fluffy, soft pillow.
It is the sound of rain falling on the ground.
It is a warning of flooding.
It is a reflector of the sky.

Laurel Dyer (9)
Kingsbury Episcopi Primary School

Eagle

He is an autumn leaf floating in the air.
He is a flash of a golden coin.
He is a tiger in the sky, swooping fast.
If he sees a mouse, he will dive down to catch his prey.
He is a rocket, speeding through the clouds.

William Stainer (9)
Kingsbury Episcopi Primary School

Cheetah

He is a dotted blanket moving around.
He is a fast killing machine as he moves from home to home.
He is a torpedo across the land.
He is a soldier, brave and fearless.
He is as hot as fire.

Kyle Butler (10)
Kingsbury Episcopi Primary School

Clouds

Clouds are a warning of rain.
Wool is a soft, fluffy cloud.
Clouds are a warning of storms.
Clouds are warm, comfortable seats.
They are fluffy, wet ice cream.
They are snowballs thrown high in the sky.
They are a king-sized bed, puffy and cosy.
Clouds are bags of rain, waiting to spoil the day.

Hannah Stuckey (10)
Kingsbury Episcopi Primary School

Leopard

He is a burglar sneaking in at night.
He is a spotty bed cover.
He is a fast car.
He is a heater starting up.
He is a criminal in the jungle killing things.

Jordan Cave (9)
Kingsbury Episcopi Primary School

The Man In The Cave

There was an old man called Dave,
He wanted to live in a cave,
'No! No!' Cried his wife,
'I would hate such a life.'
Of course, they got a divorce
And she ran off on a black and white horse,
And Dave, stayed in the cave,
With his butler, and his slave.

Steven Wride (10)
Lancaster House School

My Journey Across A Rainbow

My journey across a rainbow
Was really quite exciting
Colours glistened with a glow
Making it enticing.

On the way I met a bat,
Some beautiful fairies,
A purple cat.
I saw a bear whose name was Nerys.

Although I've got to go back home,
Past the stars and past the moon,
Through the lovely icy dome,
I better hurry it's almost noon.

I'll never forget the fun I've had
Playing with all my great new friends.
I wonder if I'll return one day?
It really just depends.

Charlotte Perry (10)
Lancaster House School

My Mischievous Chinchilla

My mischievous chinchilla,
Whose name happened to be Tilla,
Was soft and grey
And I liked the way . . .

. . . She ran about
Without a doubt,
That she might get caught -
That wasn't her thought.

But mine it was,
The reason because,
She might get lost,
And then with the cost,

Of another chinchilla,
Exactly like Tilla.

Cara Williams (9)
Lancaster House School

Our Trip

We drove to Dover,
To catch the ferry,
We didn't go under, we went over,
Chat, chat, chat, everyone was merry.
Lots of children were on this trip,
Sent by Leukaemia Research and CLIC,
Going to see Mickey Mouse and friends,
Lots of driving and lots of bends.
We sat nearly at the back,
Behind us was Sam Book and Sister Nat.
Staying in the hotel Mercuré,
Parents and children are tired for sure.
Croissants and coffee start a new day,
Off to Disneyland to go and play.
Mickey and Minnie, Goofy and Co
What a *magical* place to go.
Treatment and medicine all forgotten,
Magic and fantasy, nothing rotten.
Rides for the big, rides for the small,
This *really* is a place for all.

Sam James (10)
Lancaster House School

The Moon

The silver moon glows like a very bright light,
It hangs in the dark sky
Lighting up the night.

The white ghost, the barn owl, flies silently by,
The magical bird of the night sky.

The flitting bats fly mysteriously past my view of the moonlight,
If I did not know what they were they would give me a fright.

Zoë Rose Howell (11)
Lancaster House School

The Rainbow

At the end of the rainbow is a pot of gold,
Oh, I wish I could hold that pot of gold.

I've tried to reach the end of the rainbow
But how I'll find it, I just don't know.

I've searched in the sun and I've searched in the rain,
I've look up the street and I've look down the lane.

I've looked in the country and I've looked in the town,
I've looked far and wide, and I've looked up and down.

When I find that gold I'll be rich as a king,
I'll have fine clothes and a diamond ring.

Servants and maids and a palace for me!
But with all these riches will I really be free?

Is it really money that we need to find
Or should other things be on our minds?

Like the love and happiness of family and friends,
That's what my rainbow should have at its end.

Sophie Mussett (9)
Lancaster House School

Space

I sit here wondering if there is life out there,
Has it got a nose, has it got some hair?
Is it big-headed with pointy ears?
When it travels to Earth does it take years?

Do they live on Pluto, Jupiter or Mars
Or is it another planet further than the stars?
Do they live in houses, igloos or tents?
Do they spend Euros, Dollars or cents?

Are they smarter or dumber than us?
Do they know how to drive a bus?
Are they purple, green or red?
Do they know how to make their bed?

Do they play rugby, golf or football?
Are they fat or skinny, short or tall?
I wonder if we will ever find out
If there are aliens about?

Ben Emsley-Frake (10)
Lancaster House School

The North Pole

A polar bear on the ice
like a child going down a wet slide.
A fish in the sea
like a necklace in a jewellery box.
A penguin catching fish
like a cat pouncing on its toy.
A blue whale swimming in the sea
like an Olympic runner going for the gold.
A killer whale catching seals
like a child playing tag.
A snow dog howling
like a noisy train.

Charlotte White (10)
Monteclefe CE (VA) Junior School

Zoo Animals

The lizard is in the tree
like a pencil on a tightrope.

The parrot is in the sky
like the Northern Lights at night.

A monkey in the trees
like an acrobat on swings.

The elephant is in the jungle
like a lump of wall in a battlefield.

The giraffe is standing in the savannah
like a lamp post in the park.

The zebra is galloping in the desert
like a runner in the marathon.

The tiger is spying on its prey
like James Bond on a mission.

The lion is chasing its prey
like two children playing tag.

Alexander Mitchell (11)
Monteclefe CE (VA) Junior School

Pets

The rabbit is in its hutch
like a hot-water bottle in your bed.
The dog in its basket
like a bookmark in its book.
The cat on the sofa, asleep
like a bag of wool clutched together.
The hamster in its spinning wheel,
like the ticking of the clock.
A mouse scuttling around looking for cheese
like leaves rustling around outside by the wind.
A fish in its tank
like a soft wave on the beach.
A tortoise hibernating
like a warm jumper on a child.

Philippa Cattle (10)
Monteclefe CE (VA) Junior School

The Countryside

The cows in the field,
like patches on a quilt.

The sheep in the meadow,
like a big fluffy pillow on a bed.

The woodpecker in the trees,
like a jackhammer in a workman's hand.

The pigs in the mud patch,
like stinky pink jackets in a dustbin.

Rabbits running in the grass,
like a racing car on a track.

The fish are in the pond,
like people in their beds.

The massive tractor parked in the farmyard,
like a fat man sat in a chair.

A badger in its sett,
like an earring in a treasure box.

The fox in the bushes,
like a soldier camouflaged in battle.

Matthew Haines (10)
Monteclefe CE (VA) Junior School

The Animals' World

The dolphin is in the sea
like a gymnast on a pole.
The earthworm is in the soil
like an electrician laying wires.
The hamster is in its wheel
like a car driving off.
The elephant is spraying water
like a hosepipe washing cars.
The giraffe is eating leaves
like a window cleaner on a ladder.
The alligator is in the water
like a log lying on the ground.
The cat is sleeping on the bed
like a hot plate in the oven.
The dog is jumping up at you
like a tree beginning to grow.
The grasshopper is jumping up and down
like a green wine bottle on a table.
The bats are hanging from the roof
like icicles hanging from the freezer.
The parrot is repeating what you said
like a dictaphone.

Ashley Lazenbury (10)
Monteclefe CE (VA) Junior School

Movement Of Nature

A cheetah runs like a man on a motorbike.
A frog leaps high like the springs on a trampoline.
A snake slices through the grass like a knife cutting a piece of bread,
A monkey swings from tree to tree like vines.
A spider spreads his web like a knitting machine making a fine silk.
A turtle waddles like a stone being blown.
A Siberian tiger growls like a chainsaw cutting down trees.
A rat scurries like water rushing down a hill.
A cat climbs like a velociraptor clinging to a brontosaurus.

Kyran Robinson (9)
Monteclefe CE (VA) Junior School

The Fast And The Slow

A cheetah springs
like a Ferrari at its top speed.
A flock of ducks fly in formation
like the Red Arrows in perfect flight.
A kangaroo jumps up and down
like a gymnast on a trampoline.

A huge bendy, winding snake slithers
like a meander on a river.
A bear thunders through the forest
like a sumo wrestler.
A worm crawls underground
like the roots of a plant growing.

Ashley Francis (10)
Monteclefe CE (VA) Junior School

Summertime In The Forest

Morning breaks as the animals come out
like a jack-in-the-box popping up.

Flowers shoot up to the high heavens
like a gunshot in the air.

The squirrel collecting all his nuts
like a thief grabbing some money.

The fox hunting for some fresh meat
like a mother looking for her lost child.

Baby birds are being born
like a pen lid pulled off a pen.

The rabbit jumping all around
like a bouncy ball on the rampage.

The river flowing silently
like a big blue snake.

John Gay (10)
Monteclefe CE (VA) Junior School

Autumn

Bats swooping in the sky
like a black sea on a stormy night.
Piles of leaves on the ground
like small mountains against the sky.
Squirrels in their drey
like marshmallows toasting on a fire.
Frost beginning to come
like a white blanket covering the world.
Fireworks being let off
like a colourful rainbow in the sky.
Hedgehogs getting ready to hibernate
like a warm hot-water bottle in a bed.
Orange leaves on trees
like a warm sunset on a hill.
Birds flying to warmer places
like a black coat covering the moon.
Rabbits in their burrows
like hot water in a kettle.
The barn owl on the post
like a white shadow against the night.

Rosie Billenness (10)
Monteclefe CE (VA) Junior School

Spring

The deer are darting across the meadow
like restless children.
The flowers are shooting open,
like the morning sun rising.
The rabbits are hopping in the fields
like bouncing balls of fluff.
The rainbow appears in the sky
like a blur of mixed colours.
The baby birds are in their nests
like acorns in their cases.
The hedgehogs awake from hibernation
like a baby being introduced into the world.
The pheasants are strutting in the fields
like gold glinting in the sun.

Vicky Foyne (11)
Monteclefe CE (VA) Junior School

Zoo Animals

The whale in the cold sea
like a wave in a river.

The octopus' tentacles underwater
like squiggly lines floating away.

The dolphin jumping up and down
like a diver in a swimming pool.

The elephant in the water squirting
like a hosepipe washing a car.

The monkeys are swinging in the trees
like small children in a playground.

The parrot is flying above the sky
like a rainbow on a rainy day.

Samuel Stevens (10)
Monteclefe CE (VA) Junior School

Pets

The rabbit snug in its cage
like a teddy left in my bed.

The cat curled in a basket
like a ball of wool.

The parrot whistling to itself in its cage
like the wind on a cold day.

The hamster rummaging through its straw
like a rabbit digging a burrow.

The dogs barking in a kennel
like somebody telling their child off!

The fish swimming in a pond
like somebody playing tag.

Chloe Austin (10)
Monteclefe CE (VA) Junior School

The Sea

The dolphin is in the sea,
like a swimmer in the pool.
The whale is in the ocean.
like a fat man on a diving board.
The octopus is in the depths,
like jelly wobbling on a plate.
The fish are in the river,
like busy cars on the road.

Lucy-May Lewis (10)
Monteclefe CE (VA) Junior School

The Ocean

The dolphin diving out from the water,
like a high jumper, jumping over the bar.
The shark snooping around looking for food,
like a robber stealing jewels and money.
The clownfish swimming along happily,
like a rainbow in the sky.
The starfish lying in the sand,
like a light in the dark black sky.
The jellyfish moving with the tide,
like a ballerina moving across the stage.
The diver diving down deep,
like an astronaut floating in space.

George Bayles (10)
Monteclefe CE (VA) Junior School

Autumn

A hedgehog in some leaves
like an egg in a nest.

A spider in its web
like a flame on a Catherine wheel.

A jellyfish swimming in the sea
like a blancmange in a bowl.

An ostrich in a plane
like a statue in London.

A dolphin jumping waves
like a ball bouncing on the ground.

A crab on the sand
like a mummy in a tomb.

William Gandy (10)
Monteclefe CE (VA) Junior School

Spring Morning

The snow melts,
like spilt milk soaking into the ground.
The butterfly bursts out of its cocoon,
like the glow of a diamond.
Colours so bright and bold,
like a rainbow in the sky.
Squirrels in their trees, waking from their sleep,
like the sun rising to begin a new day.
Flowers peeping out of the ground,
like hands reaching out.
Pale pink blossom growing on trees,
like Christmas baubles.
Sheep grazing in the fields,
like fluffy clouds in the misty blue.
Sun, bright in the sky,
like a torch beaming down on the world.
But then spring leaves us for another whole year
and summer begins.

Danielle Bromley (10)
Monteclefe CE (VA) Junior School

Summer Days

The hedgehog in his hollow
Slowly coming awake,
Like bread, fresh from the oven
Once it's had its bake.

The vixen in her sett
Gradually waking up,
Like an engine turning on
From its dreams of luck.

As the day lazes by
The sheep graze in their field,
Like clouds in the sky
As the sun's fluffy shield.

The dogs in the farmyard
Snoozing in the shade,
Like cars in the junkyard
Soon to be remade.

Soon the light is fading
From the clear-blue sky,
Like ink running from a picture
To leave a star-strewn night.

The cats are in their corner
Curling up for bed,
Like the seeds in their flowerpots
Behind the garden shed.

Alice Jardine (10)
Monteclefe CE (VA) Junior School

Sunrise To Sunset

The rabbits are scurrying in the field
Like children getting ready for school.
The owls are slowly falling to sleep
Like the leaves falling off a tree.
The sheep are grazing in the field
Like the morning clouds rising.

The hamster is in its cage running around
Like children playing in the playground.
The cats are all curled up on the sofa
Like owls asleep in the trees.
The dogs are exercising in the park
Like bullets being fired from a gun.

The bats are flying in the garden
Like lightning shooting down.
The foxes are coming out to catch their prey
Like motorbikes darting down the road.
Rabbits are all cosy in their burrows
Like children all snug in their beds.

Rebecca Labdon (10)
Monteclefe CE (VA) Junior School

Africa

The eagle in the sky
like a plane flying past.
The giraffe on the plain
like a lamp post in London.
The dolphin is in the sea
like a bouncy ball going high.
The cows are in the field
like boulders under a cliff.
The rats in the sewer
like bowling balls in an alley.
The cheetah is on the plain
like a motorbike on the road.
The tarantula is in the mud house
like a dead flower.

Nicholas Wheadon (10)
Monteclefe CE (VA) Junior School

Autumn Time

The robin in its nest
like money in its safe.

The flowers are dying
like leaves falling off a tree.

The badger in its sett
like a child curled up in his bed.

The fox has killed a chicken
like a pen jabbing the page.

The hamster is in its bed
like an acorn in its shell.

The sheep are in the barn
like a wallet in a bag.

Josh Nicholson (10)
Monteclefe CE (VA) Junior School

Animals

A monkey upside down on a tree,
like a swing moving in the breeze.

A lion eating a fish,
like a lady holding her shopping bag.

An elephant stomping on the ground,
like a racing car racing on a track.

A giraffe tasting the leaves high on tall trees,
like a fisherman casting his line.

A zebra at the water hole drinking cautiously,
like a soldier in camouflage.

Jessica Jeffery (10)
Monteclefe CE (VA) Junior School

Seasons Of The Year

Flowers are opening,
Like butterflies spreading their wings out wide.
Bears waking from their hibernation,
Like the sunrise coming up.

Daffodils sitting in the green grass,
Like the sun sitting in the sky.
Sheep grazing on the hillside,
Like people sunbathing on the beach.

Leaves falling off the trees,
Like raindrops falling from the sky.
Birds setting off south,
Like leaves drifting away.

The burning smell of fire,
Like a captured spirit.
Snow covering the ground,
Like icing on a cake.

Megan Brickley (10)
Monteclefe CE (VA) Junior School

The Jungle

The elephant is in the jungle,
Like a brick house.
The giraffe is on the grass,
Like a tall lamp post.
The rat's tail wriggles
Like a slithering snake.
The rabbit hops around
Like a boy on a pogo stick.
The lion is on a rock
Like a statue in marble.
The eagle is in the sky
Like a plane flying low.

Lee Brown (10)
Monteclefe CE (VA) Junior School

In The Jungle

The lion in its cave,
Like a child in its bed.
The woodpecker in his tree hole,
Like a conker in its case.
A badger in its den,
Like a watch in a jewellery box.
The snake lying on the grass,
Like a hosepipe all curled up.
The cubs snuggling up,
Like children cuddling their mum.
The monkeys in their trees eating bananas,
Like children at a tea party.

Georgie-Anne Gray (10)
Monteclefe CE (VA) Junior School

Antarctica

Polar bears playing in the snow,
Like a child on the ice.

Seals swimming in the sea,
Like a boat drifting towards land.

Penguins waddling on the ice,
Like jelly on a plate.

Killer whales swimming swiftly,
Like a smoothly-moving knitting needle.

Snow rabbits hop through the snow,
Like a child on a pogo stick.

Huskies running around,
Like prisoners looking for freedom.

Ashleigh Rigden (10)
Monteclefe CE (VA) Junior School

Interesting Insects

The ant is carrying leaves,
Like a tug boat pulling a steamer.
The bees are in their hives,
Like children in their beds.
The butterfly is colourful,
Like paints on a shelf.
The caterpillar arches,
Like a loop in a roller coaster.
The ladybirds are spotty,
Like freckles on a face.
The snail's shell is swirly,
Like curls in your hair.

Chloe Burgess (10)
Monteclefe CE (VA) Junior School

How Animals Move

The cat is pouncing,
Like a slinky going down the stairs.

The dolphin dives,
Like a curled-up piece of cardboard.

The owl flies,
Like a majorette dancing.

The polar bear rolls,
Like a huge white snowball.

The dog is moving,
Like a lovely angel.

The snake moves,
Like a river meandering.

The spider moves,
Like eight pens joined together.

Anastasia Birch (9)
Monteclefe CE (VA) Junior School

Habitats

Badgers digging
Like cars getting crushed.

Birds in their nests,
Like babies in their cots.

Fish deep down in the ocean,
Like food pushed down into our bellies.

A flock of sheep in a field,
Like cars stuck in traffic.

Frogs jump from lily pad to lily pad,
Like grass swaying in the wind.

Pigs rolling in the mud,
Like a sweaty boy in his bed.

Snakes sliding through the grass,
Like water spraying out from the hosepipe.

Emily Walker (10)
Monteclefe CE (VA) Junior School

Spring Animals

Springtime starts
Like a new school year.
Baby rabbits sleeping,
Like balls of cotton wool.
Baby lambs learning to walk,
Like they are trying to ride a unicycle.
Sparrows trying to fly,
Like they're learning to drive aeroplanes.
Squirrels collecting nuts,
Like a person shopping for food.
Foals running in the wind,
Like helicopters in the sky.
Chicks walking along trying to find food,
Like a child looking for a lost toy.

Ruth Bowers (10)
Monteclefe CE (VA) Junior School

Jungle

An elephant crashes through the jungle
Like a weapon of mass destruction.
A snake slithers along the ground
Like a river meandering.
A giraffe eats from the highest trees,
Its neck snaking up like a crane.
The monkey swings around a branch
Like an Olympic athlete.
Meanwhile the lion swallows lumps of meat,
Like a bulldozer digging through soil.
Piranhas swim around in a lake
Like flesh-eating submarines.
The gorilla punches through his enemies
Like the world champion boxer.

Joe Swinson (10)
Monteclefe CE (VA) Junior School

Winter

Hedgehogs curled in a ball,
Like a spiky hairbrush on a dressing table.
Badgers hibernating in a sett.
Like a zebra crossing on the road.
Squirrels collecting nuts,
Like a person shopping as if a tornado was coming.
The ground iced up
Like a frosted freezer.
Cars not starting
Like a fire not lit.
Christmas decorations,
As pretty as a butterfly's pattern.
Rabbits jumping
Like a pogo stick.
Cats curled up by the fire
Like a stone in the sand.

Alice Burgess (10)
Monteclefe CE (VA) Junior School

The Way Animals Move

A frog jumping
Like a girl on a hopscotch.
A lion roaring
Like thunder and lightning.
A snake slithering
Like a hosepipe going wild on the grass.
A mouse squeaking
Like a creak in the door.
A hedgehog curled up
Like a hairbrush waiting to be picked up.
A lizard crawling
Like a baby crawling on the grass.
A bird flying
Like a paper aeroplane.

Samantha O'Neill (10)
Monteclefe CE (VA) Junior School

The Animal Poem

The sneaky fox jumped for his prey
Like a person being murdered.
The big great bear stood up and roared
Like a rock band playing.
The snake ate an egg
Like a mum feeding children.

The bat makes sound effects
Like a group of children screaming and shouting.
The little bird tries to fly with effort
Like a toddler trying to walk.
The rabbit jumping with ease,
Like a child's doll in a bouncer.

The mouse gnawing at bars
Like a saw digging into wood.
The rat scurrying across tar
Like a motorbike zooming across mud.
The sharks swimming through the sea
Like a hose flicking from side to side.

Ryan Head (10)
Monteclefe CE (VA) Junior School

Animals

Woolly sheep grazing in a field,
Like a soft, cosy blanket hanging from a cot.
Butterflies flying around me garden, safely and slowly,
Like flashing fireworks up in the sky.
Snakes slithering in the grass, cold and rough,
Like a hosepipe being reeled up.

Swan in the ocean soft and feathery,
Like some velvet toilet paper in your hand.
A hedgehog in a bush all rough and prickly,
Like a conker case lying on the floor.
A pony jumping over a jump,
Like a big, bouncy ball.

Holly Smith (11)
Monteclefe CE (VA) Junior School

Moving Fish

The shark is looking for prey,
Like a policeman looking for a robber.
The pufferfish turns into a spiky ball,
Like a balloon blowing up.
The dolphin is jumping in and out of the sea,
Like a bouncy ball crossing the ocean.
The whale is swimming through the sea,
Like a big truck crossing the road.
The goldfish is shining,
Like an underwater sun.

Laurence Pellegrinelli (11)
Monteclefe CE (VA) Junior School

Animals

The frogs leap up high,
Like a gymnast on a trampoline.
The goldfish is swimming,
Like a girl in a swimming pool.
The tadpoles are hatching in the pond
Like a chick hatching in the yard.
The newt is crawling through the grass,
Like a baby crawling out into the garden.
All these animals are so pretty,
What would we do without them?

Keziah Scott (11)
Monteclefe CE (VA) Junior School

Animals In Summer

The ponies are grazing quietly
Like a baby sleeping.

The horse's skin is
Like tree bark.

A cow is spotty
Like a pair of boxer shorts.

A sheep is
like a woolly coat.

A hedgehog is
Like a hairbrush.

The goats are milked
Like a baby feeding.

Lois Holden (9)
Monteclefe CE (VA) Junior School

Animalistic

The lion wears his mane
Like it's his own fur coat.
The tiger's thin black stripes
Look like grass than can float.

A big bear stands up
Like a human putting on mousse.
A snake slithers
Like a hose left loose.

The wolf's long howl
Is like an audience's clap,
And a scorpion lies
Like he's having a nap.

Lewis Taylor (10)
Monteclefe CE (VA) Junior School

Wildlife

The soft feathers of a colourful bird,
Like snowflakes melting in your hand.
The soft padding on a monkey's paw,
Like soft icing on a cake.
The snake is in a hole,
Like a bookmark in a book.
The seal is in the water,
Like the reeds in the pond.
The rough skin of an elephant,
Like the paper on the wall.
The scaly fish in the pond,
Like a smooth sequin in the box.
A big clump of fur this furry cat has,
Just like the carpet in your big, big class.

Sophie Farmer (9)
Monteclefe CE (VA) Junior School

The Jungle

A monkey swinging from tree to tree
like the washing drying on the line.
The giraffes standing up straight
like a lamp post in the street.
Meerkats standing watch
like soldiers guarding a fort.
A bat hanging upside down
like Hallowe'en decorations.
A hippo in the mud
like a fat lady at a health farm.
A tortoise walking in the long grass
like a baby starting to crawl.

Luke Lavender (10)
Monteclefe CE (VA) Junior School

Sunset

Sunset oh sumptuous sunset,
Glorious colours shine
Into these squinting eyes of mine.
Like a marble mist,
Brilliant things about it, I can easily list.

Sunset, oh sumptuous sunset,
Orange, pink, yellow and red.
'It's the best part of the day,' my mother said.
I feel great when I see this magnificent sight
But it's a shame when it falls into a starry night.

Sunset, oh sumptuous sunset,
Though we mustn't wish the day away.
The sunset is luxurious, I must say.
It wraps me in its soft amber blanket, I won't want less.
I feel alone when it slips away and leaves us with only darkness.

Sunset, oh sumptuous sunset.

Jess Lawrence (9)
Neroche Primary School

Monday's Tyres

Monday's tyres are in deep snow,
Start the engine up and away we go!

Tuesday's tyres are handy for gravel,
Let's get in the car and we shall travel.

Wednesday's are soft and wet,
We'll race like mad and a trophy we'll get!

Thursday's tyres are useful for asphalt,
Over a stone your car shakes to a halt.

Friday's tyres are soft or thin,
Start the race and the season will we'll win!

Saturday's tyres are snow or ice,
Each slit measures almost two woodlice.

Sunday's tyres are made by Pirelli,
With good suspension you'll wobble like jelly!

Oscar Everard (8)
Neroche Primary School

Tiger

He hangs around at quarter to one,
waiting for all the people to be gone.
Then he gets ready for his gruesome kill,
watching his prey, not moving, just still.
He walks closer and closer on his velvet paws,
then he begins to run, bringing out his claws.
He starts to speed, jumping over a boat,
jumps on his prey, digging his fangs into the throat.
The tiger's got him down, crushing his head,
the horrible old hunter, but now he's dead.

The tiger waits for his prey,
Waiting, waiting night and day!

Natalie Aicken (9)
Neroche Primary School

My Puppy Molly

My puppy Molly
is six months old,
she's really cute
and can be as good as gold.

Her coat is soft and fine,
her eyes are chocolate-brown,
her nose is always twitching
and sniffing all around.

She enjoys country walks,
she always leads the way.
Across the fields we go,
but by my side she stays.

My puppy Molly
has really sharp teeth.
She can be quite a handful
and gives me lots of grief.

My puppy Molly loves her toys,
and she loves to play.
She's my special friend
and she really makes my day.

Joanne Johnson (10)
Neroche Primary School

The Tornado

The tornado spins round and round,
and sucks everything off the ground.
The tornado spins round and round,
and after it's gone, nothing is found.

With no warning it will come,
as greedy as ever to get food for its tum.
With no warning it will come,
any day, so don't be dumb.

Do watch out, it has very good hearing,
be very careful of where it's steering.
Do watch out, it has very good hearing,
or your town will have a great clearing.

It speaks in a language you won't understand,
it whistles as it destroys the land.
It speaks in a language you won't understand,
it reaches down with a massive hand.

Maria Pablo (10)
Neroche Primary School

The Run

(The Junior Great North Run)

Running,
Run down the road,
Jog towards the finish,
Meet the family and friends,
The run.

Jenny Kerr (9)
Neroche Primary School

Clouds

The clouds are upset, drip, drip
The clouds are angry, crish, crash
The clouds are playing, slide, slip
The clouds are mad, slish, slash
The clouds are snoring, swish, swosh
The clouds are silent . . .
The clouds are running, swoo, smash.

Ryan Baker (10)
Neroche Primary School

My Hen

My egg,
round, brown, warm,
speckled, with life inside.
Day one, day two . . .
turning, turning.
Day sixteen . . .
turning, turning.
Day twenty-one . . .
chip, chip, chip . . . a head, a body,
a wet, slimy creature emerges.

My chick,
small, round, brown and black,
wobbles, falls, stands.
No feathers yet,
pecks, scratches,
growing, growing.
Getting bigger and bigger,
growing, growing,
getting feathers now,
no longer a chick.

My hen,
brown and speckled,
floppy single comb, bright red,
pecking, scratching,
clucking, clucking, laying.
One egg, two eggs, three eggs.

My egg.

Guy Wilson (10)
Neroche Primary School

Fear

Fear is as black as a night in a forest alone.
Fear smells like your loved ones are in pain.
Fear looks like a big black cloud carrying a storm.
Fear tastes like the blood splattered of thousands lost in a war.
Fear is as hard as a cold wall in the winter.
Fear reminds me of being lost in the harshest blizzard.
Fear makes me feel like my parents are dying a gruesome death.
Fear sounds like the screams of children in pain.
Fear makes my body quake and scream.
Fear is like a horrible blood-sucking monster draining me.

James Dunn (9)
Neroche Primary School

Insects

S pider, spider sneaking about
P ossibly, if I see you, I'll scream and shout.
I know you'll do me no harm,
D on't you have a scary charm.
E arly in the morning sun
R eally the sight of you will make me run.

S lithering, slimy
N ormally grimy
A lways eating my veg
I 'll make you sign a vegetable pledge
L ettuce goes missing, it's your fault, I'll sprinkle
         you down with a nice pinch of salt.

B utterfly, butterfly how you fly
U nder the cloudless bright blue sky
T he way you land on a sweet red rose
T he way you sit for a peaceful doze
E verywhere you glide around
R ainbow wings make no sound
F luttering, fluttering every day
L azy feelers, gentle way
Y ou really know how to make me glad
         when I fell so very sad.

Elizabeth Slow (10)
Neroche Primary School

Little Brats!

My mum says I'm a pain in the bottom
But I'm hoping those feelings will be forgotten
I will try to be good
Like she said that I should
Otherwise I'll get a smack round the bottom

Dad says that I'm worse than his dog
Mum thinks I eat like a hog
I will try to be good
I know that I should
But whoops! I just fell in a bog

I live on a farm
And I'm strong in the arm
I'm no good with a pen
But give me a hen
And I'll see she comes to no harm

This weekend's been pouring with rain
And we've got a new puppy to train
We've walked her for miles
And climbed over stiles
But she still can't help being a pain

Come rain, snow or sun
She must fetch from the gun
But Dad's shouts, she just cannot hear
And game she won't bring anywhere near
As all she wants is to have fun

I prefer shooting to watching the telly
Whilst out beating I've just lost a welly
I had lunch at the pub
And ate loads of grub
Now it's time for bed and I'm smelly!

Francis Bere (10)
Neroche Primary School

Camel

Feet, clumpy
Back, lumpy
Ride, bumpy
Knees, lumpy
Mood, grumpy
An' not much use to Humpty Dumpty!

Jake Gilmore (10)
Neroche Primary School

The House Of The Living Dead

The haunting wind blows,
like a screech in your ear,
the curious noise,
makes people fear.

Down in the basement,
if you dare walk around,
the evil spirits
will follow you around.

Up in the attic,
the floorboards creak,
the Devil is there,
having a sleep.

Now I advise you,
not to enter,
something might happen,
on this little adventure.

Zoe Smith (10)
Neroche Primary School

The Monsoon

Living in the rainforest,
To carry water, he's employed,
He huffs and heaves all the way,
A job not enjoyed.

His swirling hands swoop everywhere,
His fluffy grey hair sweats,
Spraying the water everywhere,
'On my foggy toes!' he frets.

The monsoon is near his journey's end,
He will be off to bed,
After traipsing on whooshing feet,
He's off to rest his head.

When he stops his snoring,
He will repeat the process,
To carry water all over again,
Trying again to control his stress.

The monsoon is complaining,
He will be sacked so soon,
His boss will not be happy,
Retirement day for Monsoon.

Sam Lawrence (11)
Neroche Primary School

My Bedroom,

I love my pink bedroom
Although it is a mess
My mum said, 'Please clean it!'
I said, 'Yes, yes, yes!'
I pack away my clothes and shoes
Quick, my mum is coming!
All away, *phew, phew, phew.*

Jodie Cox (9)
Neroche Primary School

Frodo

He sits in his cage, watching,
My furry friend,
Twitches his whiskers,
My furry friend.

He loves his food,
My furry friend,
Fills his pouches full,
My furry friend.

He plays all night,
My furry friend,
His wheel wakes up Dad,
My furry friend.

His beautiful brown fur,
My furry friend,
Always so sleek and sweet,
My furry friend.

I love to play with him,
My furry friend,
So who is he?
My hamster of course!

Lil Patuck (10)
Neroche Primary School

What Has Happened To Puppy?

What has happened to Puppy, Father?
What has happened to Pup?
I am looking all over the house

Why is there no trace of her, Father?
I can't find her anywhere
I've looked upstairs and downstairs
Why don't you listen? Don't you care?

Why hasn't her food been eaten, Father?
And her water has been stale for ages
Is she out in the garden playing?
And where are her cages?

Steffi Watts (9)
St Paul's CE (VC) Junior School, Shepton Mallet

What Has Happened To Eddy?

What has happened to Eddy?
What has happened to Ed?
I really can't find him, Daddy
And there's nothing left in his bed

Why has Eddy gone, Daddy?
His food has not been touched
I have looked high and low, Daddy
And I miss him very much.

Katie Davies (9)
St Paul's CE (VC) Junior School, Shepton Mallet

What Has Happened To Misty?

What has happened to Misty, Daddy?
What has happened to Mist?
The nice red blanket is still there
She never ever hissed.

I have checked all over, Daddy
She's not on the bed or under it
I haven't seen her for ages, Daddy
Come on, she only bit.

Tell me where she is, Daddy
I haven't seen any of her hair
Help me look for her, Daddy
Don't you care?

Chloe Mason (9)
St Paul's CE (VC) Junior School, Shepton Mallet

What Has Happened To Smudge?

What has happened to Smudgey, Mum?
What has happened to Smudge?
I checked the hutch, Mum,
All I can find is his friend Fudge.

The food is only half touched,
He's nowhere to be seen,
Are you helping me, Mum?
If not, you're mean.

Ryan Burr (9)
St Paul's CE (VC) Junior School, Shepton Mallet

What Has Happened To Freddy?

What has happened to Freddy, Mummy?
What has happened to Fred?
His bananas have not been touched,
And he's not in his bed.

What has happened to Freddy, Mummy?
He is not in a tree.
He has not tidied his room, Mummy,
He has not eaten his tea.

Robert Wearn (9)
St Paul's CE (VC) Junior School, Shepton Mallet

The Magnificent Elephant

My elephant is like the great big raincloud coming overhead,
ready to burst.
His step is like the rhino's roar when he charges.
His tusks are as white as the snowman in my garden in the winter.
His toes look like coal in my barbecue in the summer.
His trunk is as curly as a piglet's tail.

Gabriella Winter (11)
St Paul's CE (VC) Junior School, Shepton Mallet

My Magnificent Elephant

My elephant is as grey as smoke from chimneys
His ivory tusks are as white as wood ash
His eyes are as blue as a turquoise stream
His roar is that of 12 jet planes taking off
When he is angry his eyes go as red as fire
He goes as fast as a double-decker bus
His trunk is as long as a grass snake
He is as long as a Renault Espace
His skin is as rough as sandpaper
His tusks are as sharp as swords
His skin is as ruffled as an un-ironed shirt
His ears are as large as bed sheets.

Joseph Ware (10)
St Paul's CE (VC) Junior School, Shepton Mallet

My Magnificent Elephant

My elephant is grey like the sparkling moon.
His big black eyes are like the midnight sky.
He is wrinkled like creased ironing.
He is smooth and sleekly solid.
His trumpet is like a big brass band banging.
His ears flap away like flies.
His feet thump like thunder.
His toenails are tiny.
His tail hovers like a helicopter.

Katie Green (10)
St Paul's CE (VC) Junior School, Shepton Mallet

Crazy Teacher

My teacher is crazy,
My teacher is mad,
She's gone to the circus which is really bad.

She loves to do stunts,
She hates to be boring,
You'll never catch her sleeping or snoring.

My teacher is missing,
My teacher is gone,
Then we found out she's gone to Hong Kong.

Georgia Short (9)
St Paul's CE (VC) Junior School, Shepton Mallet

What Has Happened To Ted?

What has happened to Teddy, Brother?
What has happened to Ted?
There's nothing in his special place
Except his bowl and bed.

Why is his bone untouched, Brother?
The dog flap banging in the wind?
Why is there a mark where the food bowl used to be
And the food all around the bin?

Samuel Bassett (9)
St Paul's CE (VC) Junior School, Shepton Mallet

What Has Happened To Ted?

What has happened to Teddy, Brother?
What has happened to Ted?
There's nothing in his special place,
Except his bowl and bed!

Why is his bowl still full, Brother?
And why is his ball inside?
And why is the gate opening and closing?
And he's still not there, outside!

Why are you not bothered, Brother?
Why are you not fussed?
Why are you not caring?
Our poor little Ted is lost!

Rebecca Porter (9)
St Paul's CE (VC) Junior School, Shepton Mallet

Monkeys

Swingers
Cheeky players
Bananas in the trees
Picking fleas and jumping around
Monkeys.

Lucy Chaplin (9)
St Paul's CE (VC) Junior School, Shepton Mallet

Sunset

Sunset
Brown and yellow
Different shaped leaves
Trees are swaying in the wind breeze
Autumn.

Matthew Hatcher (9)
St Paul's CE (VC) Junior School, Shepton Mallet

Middle Age War (Mythical)

Swords clashing
Hammers bashing
Shields shining
Helmets falling
Armies dying
Titans crushing
Gods fighting.

Anders Pfyl (10)
St Paul's CE (VC) Junior School, Shepton Mallet

Tiffana

The icy-blue tiger,
Who's got paws as big as a tree stump,
The colour of the sky,
And stripes as dark as the moonlit sky,
Eyes as small as marbles,
He's got ears that move like an owl's head.

Lauren Hill (10)
St Paul's CE (VC) Junior School, Shepton Mallet

Matrix

Backflips
gunfire
slow motion
action fighting
punching, kicking
road scenes
people screaming
in fright
but the
good guys
always win
and the
bad guys
go down.

Peter Key (10)
St Paul's CE (VC) Junior School, Shepton Mallet

Football

F ree kick taker
O verhead kicker
O ne star striker
T otal penalty taker
B all skill champion
A ustria are losing
L oving every minute
L ove isn't in it.

Sam Jones (10)
St Paul's CE (VC) Junior School, Shepton Mallet

Horses

Fast and furious,
galloping by.
Tail waving,
to the passers-by.
Neighing to the wind,
as he cries.
Thundering across,
the open sky.

Kirsty Ames (10)
St Paul's CE (VC) Junior School, Shepton Mallet

My Magnificent Elephant

My magnificent elephant is as tall as the church's tower,
as fat as two oak trees together,
his skin is as rough as sandpaper,
he is as grey as lead in your pencil,
he is as tough as three school bullies put together.

Aimée Barnstable (10)
St Paul's CE (VC) Junior School, Shepton Mallet

Pylons

Like

a

b
l
g
g
r
l
z
z
l
y

monster
that's just eaten lots of
grime

t
h   g
a   o
t   t
's

slime hanging
off his arms and legs.
It's as dull

a

s

t

h

e

thundering
t   s
h
g   k
i
n   y.

Darcie Pritchard (10)
St Paul's CE (VC) Junior School, Shepton Mallet

Knights

Riding on horses to battle, over bridges they go.
Riding on horses to fight a horrible dragon and save a lovely princess.
Riding on horses they go, to joust in a tournament, but will they
                                                    die or not?
Firing arrows to win just a simple cup, but will they win or will they lose?
Riding on horses they go, fighting in battles with swords,
                                        spears and shields
But they may die trying to save their country and their simple homes.
Riding on horses they go, back to their simple homes
After doing all of what they had to and some more
But now they have to go over bridges again from the battle
Back to the place that they call home.

Jason Faulkes (10)
Wells Central CE Junior School

Sea

Swishy, wishy
Waves crash upon the shore
Fishing boats are bobbing more
Swishy, wishy
Scuttling crabs run to the sea
Silky sand beneath me
Swishy, wishy
Eye-catching shells lying on the sand
Multicoloured bucket and spade in each hand
Swishy, wishy
Sharp, jagged rocks that appear from the waves
Drifting seaweed that hides in the caves
Swishy, wishy
Swishy, wishy.

Thomas Orton (10)
Wells Central CE Junior School

As I Sat Under The Tree

As I sat under the tree,
A pixie came up to me.
'How do you do?' she said to me,
As I sat under the tree.

As I sat under the tree,
A little gnome came up to me.
'Good day for fishing!' he said to me,
As I sat under the tree.

As I sat under the tree,
A little imp came up to me.
'Would you like to play with me?'
As I sat under the tree.

As I sat under the tree,
A small fairy came up to me.
'You're very tall!' she said to me,
As I sat under the tree.

As I sat under the tree,
My mum and dad came up to me.
'Why are you sleeping under the tree?
Anyway, it's time for tea!'

Jay Semmler (10)
Wells Central CE Junior School

A Winter's Night

Trees sway like ships on the sea entering a deadly mist.
The leaves rustle and fall to the ground.
As I walk, the last few leaves crunch beneath my feet.
The air is as cold as ice cubes in a gigantic freezer.
The rivers, frozen, as I remember happy memories of being
a child again.
The wind howls around me like a tornado of winter's air.
Finally I turn back - my knees covered in snow, sending a painful
shiver down my spine.
My face as pale as the frost.
My hands numb and frozen as I stuff them in the warmth
of my pockets.
I could have been gone forever, if the trees kept swaying, if the
leaves kept falling,
If the air stayed cold and the rivers stayed frozen.
Lost . . . lost in the bleak, bitter wilderness.

David Hart (10)
Wells Central CE Junior School